Whi

Quick Reference

Glossary

Racial Literacy Tool

The Spirit of White Supremacy

by

Veronica Gunn

!Kaye Kaye

Whitabetes Foundation

2024

B

BARNOR HESSE'S 8 TYPES OF WHITE PEOPLE

Barnor Hesse, Associated Director of African American Studies, Political Science and Sociology identified 8 Different types of white people.

TYPES

- **White Supremacist** Clearly marked white society that preserves, names and values white supremacy
- **White Voyeurism** Wouldn't Challenge a white supremacist desires non-whiteness because its interesting, pleasurable; seeks to control the

consumption and appropriation of non-whiteness; fascination with culture (ex: consuming Black culture without the burden of Blackness)

- **White Privilege** May critique supremacy, but a deep investment in questions of fairness/quality under the normalization of whiteness and the white rule; sworn goal of 'diversity'
- **White Benefit** Sympathetic to a set of issues but only privately; won't speak/act in solidarity publicly because benefiting through whiteness in public (some POC are in this category as well)
- **White Confessional** Some exposure of whiteness takes place, but as a way of being

accountable to POC after; seek validation from POC

- **White Critical** Take on board critiques of whiteness and invest in exposing/marking the white regime; refuses to be complicit with the regime; whiteness speaking back to whiteness.
- **White Traitor** Actively refuses complicity; names what's going on; intention is to subvert while authority and tell the truth at whatever cost; need them to dismantle institutions.
- **White Abolitionist** Changing institutions, dismantling whiteness, and not allowing whiteness to reassert itself.

<u>C</u>

COLONESE LANGUAGE SCENERIOS AND TRANSLATIONS:

WHAT INDIVIDUALS STATE	WHAT IS HEARD
"I think anyone can be racist."	"I will devalue the struggles of others on the basis of race by stating everyone can experience."
"My spouse is Black."	"I will use sexual interactions with a Black person to validate racism/antiblackness aka tokenism."
"I was raised to love and	"I am a person who adheres to the Eurocentric social

respect everyone regardless of color"	standards of White supremacy through blatant disregard of acknowledging individuals' race."
"My grandchildren are biracial/mixed "	"My tokens are Black, therefore I can't be racist."
"I see no color."	"I don't want to see my own racism/White supremacy."
"Educate me."	"I want free labor."
"If we stop talking about it, it will go away."	"I need and want to ignore abuse and trauma to avoid accountability."

"Why are you so aggressive?"	"I believe in stereotypes of anti-blackness and instead of acknowledging my personal triggers, I lean into microaggressions to blame others."
"It is just hair." (white women appropriating cultural braids)	"Since I as a White women do not experience hair related oppression, I will disacknowledge the cultural importance and actual discrimination that happens for Black and POC for wearing cultural hairstyles. I will

	also garner sympathy and support as brave for choosing to appropriate these styles."
"I am 1/64th Indigenous."	"I am taking ownership of generational rape to perpetuate entitlement to a heritage that bestows minority status. This impresses the idea that I am also oppressed, equal, or as cultural inclined as actual indigenous counterparts. In stating this I also believe in blood

	quantum and Eugenics because it allocates my title of indigeneity."
"I love chocolate men"	"I fetishize men on the basis of skin color therefore contributing the historical connotations of Black men and men of color being a delicacy of sexual conquest and feast as I compare them to an edible substance."
"You have a victim mentality"	"As a victimizer, I don't understand what victim mentality means, but I will use it as a

	label when Black people and POC acknowledge their oppression. I will claim they choose their situation rather than face real oppression."
"You are anti-white"	"You want to destroy White supremacy."
"Diversity, equity and inclusion (DEI) is racist"	"I feel threatened by diversity, equity, and inclusion because it destroys the fabric and aesthetic of White supremacy in various avenues."
"I'm proud to be white."	"I take pride and ownership of all the cultural

	exploitation, destruction, abuse, and degradation that the cultural impacts of White supremacy and colonialization have created globally through the description of racial "Whiteness" and "purity".
"You talk white."	"You speak in a way that I cannot categorize as the stereotypical speech patterns associated to Black and Brown individuals. Therefore, I contribute anything in my measure of "right" or correct to

	established hierarchies of whiteness, even speech annunciation, tone, and sound."

<u>D</u>

DEFINITIONS AND APPLICATIONS

DARVO (Deny-Attack-Reverse-Victim & Offender)

DARVO represents a manipulative tactic employed by individuals feeling threatened or confronted with criticisms or complaints about their actions. Utilized by many individuals with traits of narcissism, abuse, and manipulation; this strategy enables the perpetrator to evade responsibility, silence the victim, maintain power and control, and uphold their self-image. DARVO constitutes emotional abuse, gaslighting, and the posture of playing the victim.

EXAMPLE:

In the context of cultural hairstyles, DARVO unfolds in several stages. Initially, Black individuals are denied the right to wear their cultural hairstyles. This denial is often accompanied by attacks through policies and violence. Subsequently, the perpetrators claim to be the victims of discrimination when faced with resistance. Finally, they label the victims as offenders for wearing hairstyles associated with white culture (straight, blonde, Viking knots). This tactic has been proven to propagate further discrimination within the larger context of religious discrimination.

Discrimination **THE ACTION behind the System/machine**

Discrimination refers to the action behind the system/machine. It means to make a difference in treatment or favor on a basis other than individual merit; discrimination outlook, action, or treatment, such as racial discrimination.

Inherent

Pertains to characteristics involved in the constitution or essential nature of a thing, traits that belong by nature or habit.

EXAMPLES:

- White children raised on a plantation inherently understand that "white" means free, perpetuating the removal of their collective humanity.
- White male children inherently understand that they can get away or retain small amounts of accountability for crimes such as the murder of Black individuals, disorderly conduct, or domestic violence of their own race.
- White women inherently understand that the only people socially accepted to cause them harm are white men.

- Society inherently believes that the standard of beauty is skinny, white, and blonde.
- White people inherently believe that Black people are more violent.
- It's inherent that you will get wet if you jump in the pool.

Inherit

To receive from a predecessor, obtain from someone after their death, or receive by genetic transmission.

EXAMPLE

- When a parent dies, the child will inherit their jewelry and generational wealth.

Prejudice (pre-judge) <u>THE MINDSET</u> behind the Action

Prejudice encompasses the formation of an adverse opinion or bias **WITHOUT** just grounds or prior experience to acquiring sufficient knowledge. It also denotes an irrational attitude of hostility directed towards an individual, a group, a race, or their perceived characteristics. Prejudice, or pre-judging, constitutes the cognitive disposition underlying actions. It represents the infliction of injury or harm resulting from the judgment or action of another, disregarding one's rights.

Racial Macro-Aggression

Racial macro-aggressions refers to evident and systemic forms of racial discrimination and oppression directed at individuals or groups based on their race or ethnicity.

- Racial profiling by law enforcement agencies targeting specific racial or ethnic groups for heightened scrutiny and suspicion.
- Institutionalized discrimination in housing, education, or employment that systematically disadvantages certain racial or ethnic groups.
- Denial of basic human rights, such as voting rights or access to healthcare, based on race or ethnicity.
- Policies and practices that perpetuate racial segregation and inequality, such as redlining or gerrymandering.
- Hate crimes and acts of violence motivated by racial bias, including racially motivated assaults or acts of vandalism.

- Systemic disparities in the criminal justice system, including racial disparities in arrest rates, sentencing, and incarceration rates.
- Economic exploitation and discrimination, such as unequal pay or employment opportunities based on race or ethnicity.
- Cultural appropriation and the exploitation of cultural symbols, practices, or traditions without proper acknowledgment or respect for their origins.

Racial Micro-Aggression

Racial microaggressions are brief and commonplace daily verbal, behavioral, or environmental indignities, whether intentional or unintentional, that communicate hostile, derogatory, or negative racial slights and insults toward people of color. Perpetrators of microaggressions are often unaware that they engage in such communications when they interact with racial/ethnic minorities.

EXAMPLES OF RACIAL MICRO-AGGRESSIONS:

- Following a Black customer around the store (also known as racial profiling).
- Asking to touch a Black person's hair or doing it without asking.
- Assuming a Black college student is on an athletic scholarship.
- Saying, "You are so well spoken/articulate".
- Asking, "Where are you really from?"

- Saying, "I don't look at you as a Black person. You are different."
- Expecting the one [insert marginalized group] person to lead [racialized/marginalized group] History/Awareness/Culture Appreciation Month.

Racism <u>THE SYSTEM/MACHINE causing harm</u>

Racism denotes the system/machine causing harm, such as the systemic oppression of a racial group to the social, economic, and political advantage of another; and/or political or social system founded on racism and designed to execute its principles.

Sundown Towns

Towns or whole counties that allow Black People to work in the area but not live; Black People risked bodily harm and/or death if they were caught inside the city/county lines at sundown.

Sundown Cities:

- **Anna, Illinois** - "Anna" is reportedly an acronym for "Ain't No N****rs Allowed," making it one of the most infamous sundown towns. It has a long history of racial exclusion.
- **Cicero, Illinois** - Known for violent resistance to integration, Cicero became notorious after the 1951

Cicero race riot, where a mob attacked an apartment building that an African American family had moved into.

- **Forsyth County, Georgia** - In the early 20th century, all African Americans were violently expelled from the county. Forsyth County remained an all-white community for decades and was known for its hostility towards Black people.

- **Sundown, Missouri** - Many towns in Missouri were known for sundown policies, with signs warning African

Americans to leave by sunset.

- **Vidor, Texas** - Notorious for its Ku Klux Klan activity and racial segregation, Vidor has been one of the most well-known sundown towns in the South.

- **Darien, Connecticut** - Known for its history of racial exclusion and being a sundown town, Darien had an unwelcome reputation for African Americans.

White Privilege

Refers to the ability to live without fear of race impacting the pursuit of happiness, wealth, and independent security within a social system.

QUESTIONS TO SEE IF YOU HAVE PRIVILEGE

- Do you experience severe anxiety when being pulled over, even if you haven't broken any laws?
- Do you contemplate corrective actions when wearing cultural hairstyles like Locs and Bantu Braids to work or school?
- Do you notice one or more employees at a store following or watching you?
- Do you fear being harmed for being white?
- Did you fear for your life when delivering your baby?

- Do you consider it racist for Black people to avoid socializing with white people due to the violence committed towards the Black community by white people?

H

HOW TO DISRUPT WHITE SUPREMACY:

Element	EXAMPLE	Disrupt
Perfectionism	Reflects a mindset where making a mistake is equated with being a mistake, and doing wrong is perceived as being wrong	Create a culture that acknowledges mistakes as pathways to

	inherently	solutions and positive outcomes.
Only One Right Way	Insistence on a singular approach akin to a missionary's belief in the supremacy of their way, rather than appreciating diverse perspectives.	Practice recognizing defensive behavior and insistence on your own way. Take a moment to breathe and

		consider alternative paths that may enhance your approach or provide what you truly need.
Paternalism	Believing you have the right to lead and looking for a fatherly figure to rescue the organization; Looking for a paternal figure to "save" an	Help individuals at every level comprehend how power

	organization/age ncy/company.	functions, their own level of authority, what it means to wield power responsibly, and how to collectively combat and recover from internalized habits of monopo

		lizing and safeguarding power.
Objectivity	Dismissing "emotional" responses while prioritizing "rational" ones.	Enhance emotional intelligence and maturity.
Sense of Urgency	Urgent deadlines set by higher management, prioritizing speed over thoroughness in decision-making processes, disregarding important	Developing realistic work plans that consider the actual experien

	perspectives or data due to exorbitant time constraint.	ces of the people and the organiza tion involve d.
Defensi veness	Due to a propensity for binary perspectives, individuals in positions of authority perceive criticism as either threatening or impolite.	Examin e the correlati on between defensiv eness and underlyi ng fears such as loss of power, loss of

		prestige, loss of comfort, and loss of privilege.
Denial	Refusing to acknowledge the historical legacy of white supremacy and racism, as well as the structural nature of racial disparities, involves rewriting, reframing, or omitting histories to erase or downplay	Consider the possibility of being incorrect.

	racism.	
Quantity over Quality/ Progress is Bigger	Discomfort with emotion and feelings, as well as the conventional definition of success as always being associated with growth in magnitude.	Differentiate between growth, which is necessary and naturally occurring, and the conditioned desire for "more" – more possessions, more

		transactional power, more influence – for its own sake.
Worship of the Written Word	The inability or refusal to acknowledge information shared through stories, embodied knowing, intuition, and the diverse range of ways we individually and collectively learn and understand	Engaging in active listening without immediately responding or engaging in debate or

	in favor of a preferred induction of White supremacy.	rebuttal.
Either/ Or	Presenting options or issues in a binary manner, framing them as either/or – good/bad, right/wrong, with us/against us.	When confronted with urgency and binary thinking, advocate for slowing down. Encourage individuals to take a

		pause, a breath, restate the goal, and explore alternative perspectives more deeply.
Power Hoarding	Individuals in positions of power may perceive suggestions for change within the organization as a threat, interpreting them as a reflection of	Incorporate power-sharing as an explicit organizational and commu

	their leadership.	nity value.
Individualism	Demanding to be seen, heard and centered as an individual instead of a participant in white supremacy.	Look for opportunities to understand people outside of yourself who have different experiences, backgrounds and culture.
Right to	White	Personal

Comfort	individuals, or those with dominant identities, sometimes equate individual acts of unfairness with systemic racism. Thus, believing entitlement to the action or emotion of support even if individual and associated identity are the cause.	growth often requires stepping outside of one's comfort zone.
Anonymity (unofficial)	Both digital and physical Ku Klux Klan (KKK) members	Consider the notion that

| | engages in harmful behavior such as commenting on Black social media or participating in panels with the intent to cause harm, disrupt Black unity, and traumatize and antagonize Black individuals from the anonymity of their residences. | deriving emotional and spiritual satisfaction from intentionally harming others designates one as a deeply troubling figure, particularly within the context of racial |

		dynamics. Recognize that the intensity of such emotions may stem from an awareness of one's own inadequacies.

R

READULIN THERAPY

Reading is required treatment and can be done with no one around. It allows a person without emotional maturity and regulation skills to throw, jump on or burn the book without anyone witnessing the severe whitabetic flair up. In addition, reading doesn't mean you can comprehend what is being said. It's suggested you look for videos of the author discussing the book or its theme. Most importantly, most have webpages where you can order books, seek advisement/coaching/therapy as well as an invaluable education that can help break down the intellectual and emotional blocks Whitabetes creates.

<u>S</u>

SEXISM VERSUS MISOGYNY

Sexism and misogyny, while related, have distinct definitions and implications. **Misogyny** refers to the systemic devaluation and denigration of those who identify as female, characterized by a deep-seated disgust and hostility toward the feminine. It involves active enforcement of patriarchal norms, particularly when these norms are threatened. **Sexism**, on the other hand, encompasses a broader set of beliefs and practices that support patriarchal social structures. It includes, but is not limited to, misogyny. While sexism maintains and perpetuates gender inequality through discriminatory attitudes and practices, misogyny specifically targets and punishes those who challenge or threaten the patriarchal system, ensuring its continued dominance. Sexism provides the ideological foundation for gender discrimination, whereas misogyny acts as a defensive mechanism to reinforce and protect this foundation against potential challenges.

SUPPLEMENTARY READING FOR BOTH TYPE A AND B WHITABETIC THERAPY

"Destruction of Black Civilization: Great Issues of a Race from 4500 B.C. to 2000 A.D."

by Chancellor Williams **(1974)**

"King Leopold's Ghost: A Story of Greed, Terror, and Heroism in Colonial Africa"

by Adam Hochschild **(1998)**

"Medical Apartheid: The Dark History of Medical Experimentation on Black Americans from Colonial Times to the Present"

by Harriet A. Washington **(2006)**

"The New Jim Crow: Mass Incarceration in the Age of Colorblindness"

by Michelle Alexander **(2010)**

- **"Stamped from the Beginning: The Definitive History of Racist Ideas in America"**

by Ibram X. Kendi (2016)

"Caste: The Origins of Our Discontents"

by Isabel Wilkerson **(2020)**

"The 1619 Project: A New Origin Story"

by Nikole Hannah-Jones **(2021)**

T

TYPE A WHITABETIC BOOK THEAPRY

"White Rage: The Unspoken Truth of Our Racial Divide"

by Carol Anderson **(2016)**

"White Fragility: Why It's So Hard for White People to Talk About Racism"

by Robin DiAngelo **(2018)**

"Rising Out of Hatred: The Awakening of a Former White Nationalist"

by Eli Saslow (2018)

"Dying of Whiteness: How the Politics of Racial Resentment Is Killing America's Heartland"

by Jonathan M. Metzel **(2019)**

• **"They Were Her Property: White Women as Slave Owners in the American South"**

by Stephanie E. Jones-Rogers **(2019)**

• **"Nice Racism: How Progressive White People Perpetuate Racial Harm"**

by Robin DiAngelo **(2021)**

TYPE B WHITABETIC BOOK THEARPY

"Post Traumatic Slave Syndrome: America's Legacy of Enduring Injury and Healing"

by Dr. Joy DeGruy **(2005)**

"Black Fatigue: How Racism Erodes the Mind, Body, and Spirit"

by Mary-Frances Winters **(2020)**

"Set Boundaries, Find Peace: A Guide to Reclaiming Yourself"

by Nedra Glover Tawwab **(2021)**

"The Unapologetic Guide to Black Mental Health: Navigate an Unequal System, Learn Tools for Emotional Wellness, and Get the Help You Deserve"

by Rheeda Walker, PhD **(2020)**

GLOSSARY

The intention behind this glossary is to compile terms frequently utilized in discussions about race and White supremacy. While this glossary represents only a small selection, these definitions, grounded in reputable sources, provide a foundational understanding for discussions about race, racism, and the broader social context of Whitabetes. These expanded definitions enhance the capacity to engage in informed discussions about white supremacy and its pervasive impact.

A

Ableism: A pervasive system of discrimination that privileges individuals without disabilities while disadvantaging those with disabilities. Ableism manifests in interactions between individuals, within institutions, social systems, and as part of societal norms, expectations, and policies. It suggests that there is a "normal" way of living where certain abilities are deemed essential for inclusion and happiness.

Accountability: The state of being responsible for the harm one causes to another or others. In discussions about race and racism, it often refers to acknowledging and addressing one's role in perpetuating racial injustices and working towards restitution and healing.

African: A person of African descent or origin; often used to refer to individuals, especially Black people, who have African ancestry and heritage.

African American Vernacular English (AAVE): A distinctive language variety spoken within the African Diaspora, originating from the Black community in the United States. AAVE has its own grammatical, phonological, and lexical patterns.

American Native or Alaska Native: A person having origins in any of the original peoples of North and South America (including Central America) who maintains tribal affiliation or community attachment.

Anonymity: The condition of being anonymous, allowing individuals to move and navigate spaces, such as social media or certain events, without revealing their identity. This can provide both protection and an avenue for unchecked behavior.

Anti-: A prefix denoting opposition or hostility toward something in opinion, sympathy, or practice.

Asian: A person having origins in any of the original peoples of the Far East, Southeast Asia, or the Indian subcontinent, including countries such as Cambodia, China, India, Japan, Korea, Malaysia, Pakistan, the Philippines, Thailand, and Vietnam.

Afrocentric: Pertaining to or influenced by African cultures or those of African origin. Afrocentric perspectives emphasize the importance and contributions of African cultures and civilizations.

Anti-Black: Contempt and/or hostility directed toward Black people. It includes systemic policies and practices that specifically target and oppress Black individuals and communities.

Example: Policies that impose restrictions on Black hairstyles, such as locs.

Asymptomatic: A person affected by a condition but displaying no symptoms.

Bias: An inclination of temperament or outlook; especially a personal and sometimes unreasoned judgment or prejudice.

Bicoon: A person with one white parent (usually the mother) and one Black parent, who exhibits anti-Black behaviors (such as colorism and featurism), ideas, and rhetoric in alignment with their white parent. (Veronica Gunn, Founder, Whitabetes Foundation).

Bigot: A person who is obstinately or intolerantly devoted to their own opinions and prejudices, especially one who regards or treats members of a group (such as a racial or ethnic group) with hatred and intolerance.

Biphobia: refers to the fear, hatred, or mistrust of bisexual people. It involves negative attitudes, stereotypes, discrimination, and prejudice specifically directed at individuals who are attracted to both males and females. Biphobia can manifest in various ways, including:

- **Denial and Erasure**: Refusing to acknowledge

bisexuality as a valid sexual orientation, often implying that individuals must be either heterosexual or homosexual.

- **Stereotyping**: Perpetuating harmful stereotypes about bisexual people, such as viewing them as promiscuous, confused, or indecisive.
- **Exclusion**: Marginalizing bisexual individuals within both heterosexual and LGBTQ+ communities, often leading to feelings of isolation
- **Discrimination and Prejudice**: Treating bisexual people unfairly in social, professional, or legal

contexts based on their sexual orientation.

- **Invisibility**: Ignoring or minimizing the presence and contributions of bisexual people in media, culture, and discussions about sexuality.

Biphobia can occur both within the heterosexual community and within the LGBTQ+ community, where bisexual people might face invalidation or discrimination from individuals who identify as either heterosexual or homosexual.

Biracial: A descriptive term for an individual whose parents are of different races.

Black (Person)/African American: A person having origins in any of the Black racial groups of Africa.

Blackface: Dark makeup worn to mimic the appearance of a Black person, especially to mock or ridicule Black people; when white individuals use dark makeup to caricature Black people in a stereotypical and derogatory manner.

Example: Minstrel shows of the 1800's, Digital TikTok filters such as a monkey or paint on face.

Blackfish: A term used to describe a non-Black person who intentionally appropriates Black culture, aesthetics, and identity, often through social media, to gain attention or monetary benefits. This behavior includes but is not limited to altering their appearance, adopting Black hairstyles, and using makeup to darken their skin tone to appear racially ambiguous or Black.

Blacoon: A person with two Black parents who suffers from Whitabetes Type B.

Blackabetes: The response by Type As and a few Type Bs to Whitabetes. This response exemplifies the intellectual, emotional, and mental blocks experienced by Type As. (Veronica Gunn, Whitabetes Foundation Founder).

Bully: An individual with greater power (physical or economic) who dominates, mistreats, torments, and abuses someone or a group that is vulnerable and possesses less power.

Bullying: Behaviors exhibited by an individual seeking to dominate, abuse, and/or torment a vulnerable person or group.

<u>C</u>

Capitalism: An economic system characterized by private or corporate ownership of capital goods, with investments determined by private decisions, and prices, production, and distribution of goods primarily influenced by competition in a free market.

Caucacity: referring to the audacity of a white person who exhibits racism, privilege, entitlement, or other inappropriate behavior (Veronica Gunn, Whitabetes Foundation Founder).

Cavefathers: a description of an individual's origin legacy as through neanderthal bequest that exhibits the physical characteristics of troglodytes and associated features.

Civil Rights: Personal rights guaranteed and protected by the U.S. Constitution and federal laws enacted by Congress.

Collectivism: The prioritization of a group's collective harmony, freedoms, liberties, and rights over an individual's emotional and mental comfort; unity, selflessness.

Colonese: The language of white supremacy that has evolved into a vernacular spoken by individuals who may not understand it but recognize its harmful impact. Commonly used and well known with honkys, Colonese is often coupled with **WAVE,** White American Vernacular English (Drop_ATL of Ubuntu Vision).

Colorism: Prejudice or discrimination within a racial or ethnic group, favoring people with lighter skin over those with darker skin.

Construct: To devise or create by clever use of imagination; to make or form by combining or arranging parts or elements.

Covert: Not in the open; concealed or hidden.

Critical Race Theory (CRT): A framework for examining the relationship between race and laws and legal institutions, particularly in the United States, emphasizing that race is a sociological rather than biological designation and that racism pervades society and is perpetuated by the legal system.

CROWN Act: The CROWN Act, which stands for "Creating a Respectful and Open World for Natural Hair," is a law prohibiting race-based hair discrimination, including the denial of employment and educational opportunities due to hair texture or protective hairstyles such as braids, locs, twists, or Bantu knots.

Culture: The customary beliefs, social forms, and material traits of a racial, religious, or social group; the characteristic features of everyday existence shared by people in a place or time; the set of shared attitudes, values, goals, and practices that characterize an institution or organization; patterns of human knowledge, belief, and behavior that rely on the capacity for learning and transmitting knowledge to succeeding generations.

Cultural Appreciation: The earnest endeavor to learn about or explore a different culture with respect, understanding, and honor, without personal gain or exploitation. This involves listening, striving to understand, and honoring the culture and its people.

Cultural Appropriation: The act of taking one aspect of a culture that is not one's own and using it for personal interest without consent, permission, or cultural context. This often leads to exploitation and a narrow view of other cultures. Specifically, it refers to when a white person uses another group's sacred culture for their own identity or profit without regard for the historical abuse committed against that culture by their forefathers.

D

DARVO (Deny-Attack-Reverse Victim-Offender): A manipulative tactic often employed by individuals when they feel threatened or confronted by criticisms or complaints about their actions. This tactic enables the perpetrator to evade responsibility, silence the victim, maintain power and control, and preserve their self-image. It is a form of emotional abuse, gaslighting, and playing the victim. Although anyone can use DARVO, it is most frequently observed in narcissistic, abusive, and manipulative individuals.

Dark White: Individuals who do not wish to identify as Black due to internalized beliefs stemming from white supremacy, or white individuals who disassociate from whiteness due to its historical association with 500+ years of oppressive behavior.

Digital Honky: An individual who invades social media spaces with the intent to cause harm.

Diversity: The inclusion of individuals from various races, cultures, and backgrounds within a group or organization.

Discriminate: To treat individuals differently based on criteria other than individual merit.

Discrimination: An outlook, action, or treatment that unfairly differentiates between people, particularly based on race.

E

Emotional: Dominated by or prone to emotion.

Equity: Fair and equal treatment for all individuals, ensuring justice and impartiality.

Ethnicity: A group of people sharing a common language, culture, and body of traditions.

Exclusion: The act of barring someone from participation, consideration, or inclusion.

Exploit: To make use of someone or something unfairly for one's own advantage.

F

False Equivalency/Comparison: A logical fallacy that occurs when one incorrectly asserts that two or more things are equivalent simply because they share some characteristics, despite notable differences between them.

Example: Comparing chattel slavery to indentured servitude; Classism compared to racism.

Fetish: An object, part of the body, or activity that typically lacks sexual connotation but induces habitual erotic response or fixation. It can also refer to unconventional sexual practices involving such objects or activities, as well as any object, idea, etc., eliciting unquestioning reverence or respect. In anthropology, it denotes an object believed to be imbued with a potent spirit or magical properties.

Example: "I love chocolate men and women." and " I want mixed babies."

Freedom: The ability to feel, think, move, talk, and breathe without restraints or fear of unprovoked violence.

G

Gaslighting: The act or practice of grossly misleading someone, often for one's own advantage. It involves the psychological manipulation of a person, typically over an extended period, causing the victim to question the validity of their own thoughts, perceptions of reality, or memories. This manipulation often results in confusion, loss of confidence, diminished self-esteem, uncertainty regarding one's emotional or mental stability, and dependency on the perpetrator.

Gender: How a person identifies themselves in terms of social and cultural roles, behaviors, and attributes considered appropriate for men and women.

Guilt: The state of having committed an offense or the feeling of responsibility for a wrong.

H

Halfrican: An individual with one African/Black parent and one non-African/Black parent.

Hispanic: Refers to people who speak Spanish or have a background in a Spanish-speaking country.

Honky: A descriptive term, often felt as derogatory, for a white person (usually a man) who invades Black spaces with the intent to antagonize, disrupt, and abuse Black people in various forms. This word also has historical connotation for White men who solicit Black individuals for sexual encounters (Veronica Gunn, Whitabetes Foundation, Founder).

Honky Heifer: A descriptive term, often felt as derogatory, for a white woman who demands authority and control over spaces that center everyone but white people. They are often associated with creating and influencing policies reminiscent of the Daughters of the Confederacy, impacting the American education system negatively (Veronica Gunn, Whitabetes Foundation, Founder).

Honkys On Acid (HOA): A term referring to groups of white people who come together to cause harm to Black people (Veronica Gunn, Whitabetes Foundation, Founder).

Examples: Historical events like the Tulsa Massacre; contemporary events like the January 6th insurrection; TikTok digital spam bots sent to disrupt Black individuals live video streams.

Honky-Tonk: a type of bar that was common in the early 20th century that generally excluded or hindered various groups of Black and Brown individuals from admission.

Human Rights: Fundamental rights that every person possesses simply by being human, regardless of nationality, sex, ethnicity, color, religion, language, or any other status. These rights range from the right to life to those that ensure a quality life, such as rights to food, education, work, health, and liberty.

I

Identity Conflict/Crisis: The experience of lacking purpose or direction in life due to an unclear understanding of one's values, passions, or spiritual connections. This often results from social constructs perpetuated by white supremacy.

Inclusion: The practice of including and accommodating people who have historically been excluded due to their race, gender, sexuality, or ability.

Individual Racism: The beliefs, attitudes, and actions of individuals that support or perpetuate racism, both consciously and unconsciously. The U.S. cultural narrative often focuses on individual racism while neglecting systemic racism.

Individualism: Prioritizing personal rights, freedoms, economic gains, and emotional and social comforts over the collective good. Proponents of the "bootstrap" theory often adhere to individualism.

Example: "I nor my family-owned slaves."

Infantilize: To treat someone as if they are an infant, including speaking to them in a condescending manner.

Example: Treating elderly individuals as incapable when they are not; acting as if young adults are aloof.

Intersectional discrimination: refers to the overlapping and interdependent systems of discrimination or disadvantage that arise when someone's identity spans multiple marginalized or oppressed groups. This concept acknowledges that people can experience discrimination in a variety of ways that intersect and compound each other, leading to unique and complex experiences of inequality.

Example: A Black transgender woman might face discrimination when seeking healthcare due to both racial bias against black people and transphobia. Healthcare providers may not understand her unique needs, leading to inadequate or discriminatory treatment. Additionally, she might encounter challenges in finding employment due to biases against both black individuals and transgender people, further limiting her economic opportunities. This intersectional discrimination highlights the compounded barriers she faces due to her dual identities.

Intersectionality: is a term coined by legal scholar Kimberlé Crenshaw in 1989 to describe how different forms of discrimination and oppression (such as racism, sexism, classism, and others) overlap and intersect in the lives of marginalized individuals or groups. Crenshaw introduced this concept to highlight how single-axis frameworks that consider race or gender in isolation fail to capture the full extent of systemic injustice and social inequality.

Key Aspects of Intersectionality

- **Multiple Identities**: Intersectionality examines how various identities (race, gender, sexuality, class, disability, etc.) coexist and interact within an individual, influencing their experiences and opportunities.

- **Compounded Discrimination**: It emphasizes that people can face multiple forms of discrimination simultaneously. For example, a Black woman may experience racism and sexism together in a way that is distinct from the experiences of white women or Black men.

- **Systems of Power**: Intersectionality acknowledges that social systems and structures of power are interconnected and cannot be understood in isolation. These systems work together to perpetuate inequalities.
- **Inclusive Analysis**: By considering the intersections of various forms of oppression, intersectionality provides a more comprehensive analysis of social issues and contributes to more inclusive and effective advocacy and policy-making.

Example: Black Transgender Women and Intersectionality

A Black transgender woman will experience workplace discrimination in ways that different from those of her white female or Black male colleagues. This can include:

- **Racial Stereotyping**: Facing racial biases and stereotypes that undermine her capabilities and contributions.
- **Gender Discrimination**: Encountering sexism, such as being passed over for promotions or being paid less than male counterparts.

- **Cultural Expectations**: Navigating cultural expectations and norms that may impose additional burdens or limitations.

Inherent: The natural or typical state of things.

Example: "If you live in a garbage dump you will inherently smell like a dirty trash can."

Inherit: To receive property or money following the death of someone.

Example: " I inherited my Peepaws shit stained Ku Klux Klan Grand Wizard robe."

Institutional Racism: Discriminatory treatments, unfair policies, or biased practices within organizations that result in inequitable outcomes favoring white individuals over people of color. These policies often do not explicitly mention any racial group but are intended to create advantages for certain groups.

Intellect: The capacity for knowledge and rational thought, distinguished from the capacity to feel and will; especially when highly developed.

Intellectual: Pertaining to the use of the intellect.

Intellectual Abuse: Disrespecting a person's learning style, way of thinking, or intellectual interests. This can include attempting to debate without adequate education or awareness, often with the intent to cause confusion and chaos.

Internalize: To incorporate values, patterns of culture, etc., within oneself as guiding principles through learning or socialization.

Interpersonal Racism: Due to structural and systemic racism, public expressions of micro or macro aggressions between White individuals and White companies, often involving slurs, biases, or hateful actions directed towards Black and POC individuals **ONLY**.

Ism: A distinctive doctrine, cause, or theory, often associated with oppressive and discriminatory attitudes or beliefs; adherence to a system of principles.

J

Jamal: a name most often given to African American individuals often used in a negative connotation for stereotype of Black aggression.

Example: telling someone, " Calm down Jamal!" Calling the individual Jamal especially if the other individuals name is not Jamal nor a Black individual.

K

Karen/Ken: White individuals who become overly emotional and unregulated, often calling the police when they see Black people engaging in everyday activities.

Klancestors: People who express similar ideology and commonalities in action or spirit to Ku Klux Klan rhetoric in both instances of familial linage and not.

L

La Raza: "La Raza" literally translates as "The Race," but it is more colloquially understood to mean "The People." It celebrates the multiracial and ethnic heritage of Latinos in the United States. The lineage of La Raza is rooted in the Spanish Conquest of the indigenous peoples of Mexico and the subsequent mestizaje, or mixed racial and ethnic identities, comprising indigenous, European, and African ancestries unique to the Americas. The Raza Studies Department at San Francisco State University describes it as referring to mestizos or mixed peoples, embodying the blood of the conquered and conqueror, including indigenous (i.e., Aztec, Mayan, Olmec, Yaqui, Zapotec, and numerous other Native Americans), European, African, and Asian heritages.

Latino(a): Refers to people from Latin America, including Central America, South America, and the Caribbean. This term, like Hispanic, does not denote race; Latinos can be White, Black, Indigenous, Asian, etc..

Latin-X: Latin-X is a gender-neutral term used to refer to individuals of Latin American descent. The term emerged as a more inclusive alternative to Latino and Latina, which are gender-specific. Latin-X aims to recognize and respect non-binary, gender-nonconforming, and transgender individuals within the Latin American community, thereby promoting inclusivity and diversity. It underscores the importance of language evolving to encompass and affirm the identities of all individuals, regardless of gender.

Liberty: The positive enjoyment of various social, political, or economic rights and privileges.

Literacy: The proficiency gained through intellectual capability.

Literate: Having intelligence or skill.

Lynching Bees: A historical term referring to the gatherings of white people, including men, women, and children, to watch the hanging and/or burning of Black individuals. These events were often viewed as a form of entertainment, with children given front-row seats to witness the torture and execution of Black individuals, leaving indelible memories of the violence through cannibalism and human taxidermy (Veronica Gunn, Whitabetes Foundation, Founder).

M

Macroaggressions: Systemic and institutionalized forms of bias and oppression that impact the lives of entire groups of marginalized people. These are embedded in policies, procedures, and practices that oppress minoritized groups, ranging from societal to institutional levels.

Example: Travel bans against people from certain countries (e.g., Executive Order 13769), the absence of representation of minoritized groups in media, and medical education curricula that reinforce power imbalances.

Manipulation: The act of controlling or playing upon someone by artful, unfair, or insidious means, often for one's own advantage.

Mantrum: A term describing when a man displays uncontrollable emotions akin to a child having a tantrum, typically occurring when they encounter intellectual challenges during debates. This behavior often reflects a refusal to accept authority and control in any space they enter (Veronica Gunn, Whitabetes Foundation, Founder).

Mental: Of or relating to the mind, particularly the total emotional and intellectual response of an individual to external reality; relating to mental activity or its products as an object of study; occurring or experienced in the mind

Mestizo: A term originally meaning "person of mixed Spanish and Amerindian parentage," derived from the Latin mixtus, or "mixed." While still used by some Latin American groups to describe their mixed heritage, it is becoming less common. Approximately one-third of people identifying as Hispanic in the U.S. also describe themselves as mestizo.

Micro-Aggression: A comment or action that subtly and often unconsciously or unintentionally expresses a prejudiced or hostile attitude toward a member of a marginalized group.

Miscegenated: refers to the act of "mixing" or being "mixed" racially, specifically through marriage, cohabitation, or sexual relations between people of different races. It describes the state or condition resulting from such racial interbreeding. Historically, the term has been used in a context that underscores racial biases and segregationist policies.

Misogyny: Hatred of, aversion to, or prejudice against women.

Misogynoir: Hatred of, aversion to, or prejudice against Black women.

Mulatto: An outdated slur representing inhumane categorization due to blood quantum and Eugenics for someone with one Black parent and one White parent.

N

Natal Sex: Assigned sex at birth based on genitalia and chromosome makeup.

Nationalism: Believing one's country is to be praised and worshipped as the "superpower".

Nationality: Membership to a particular nation.

Native Hawaiian or Other Pacific Islander: A person having origins in any of the original peoples of Hawaii, Guam, Samoa, or other Pacific Islands.

Negropean: A person from Africa or with African parents who was raised in Europe and believes there is little to no racism there; believes that Americans focus too much on race.

Nuance: A subtle distinction or variation.

O

Othering: When an American avoids identifying as one of the five races designated by the government in

America; When white people avoid identifying as white.

Example: Include saying "I am 'Merican" or "I am [insert European, Icelandic, Irish, Scillian or Nationality]" when white people do not want to say they are white. Also, "I am multi-racial."

Overt: Done openly and without shame.

P

Phobia: An unfounded fear or avoidance of an object, place, or whole group of people.

Prefer: To choose one over another.

Prejudice: To have a negative pre-judgment against an individual, group, race, or their supposed characteristics with **NO** logical reason, experience, or proof to support feelings of contempt.

Pro-Black: A concept that centers on advancing the growth, well-being, empowerment, and self-determination of Black communities.

Projection: The process of displacing one's feelings onto a different person, animal, or object. Most often used to describe defensive projection—attributing one's own unacceptable urges to another.

Example: If someone continuously bullies and ridicules a peer about his insecurities, the bully might be projecting his own struggle with self-esteem onto the other person.

Pronouns: A set of words (such as I, she, he, you, it, we, or they) utilized as substitutes for nouns. Pronouns in no way identify an individuals sexual identity or gender.

Example: "My pronouns are she/her."; "I identify as they/them."

Proximate: Very near.

Proximity: The quality or state of being proximate; closeness.

Q

Quadroon: A term used to describe Black people with one Black grandparent.

Queerphobia: refers to the fear, hatred, or discrimination against individuals who identify as queer. The term "queer" is an umbrella term used by some people to describe a sexual orientation, gender identity, or gender expression that does not conform to societal norms. Queerphobia encompasses negative attitudes, behaviors, and institutional practices directed at people who identify as LGBTQ+ or whose gender or sexual identity falls outside traditional categories. Queerphobia can manifest in various forms:

- **Homophobia**: Fear, hatred, or discrimination specifically against people who are attracted to the same sex.
- **Transphobia**: Fear, hatred, or discrimination specifically against transgender or gender non-conforming people.
- **Biphobia**: Fear, hatred, or discrimination specifically against bisexual people.

- **General Discrimination and Prejudice**: Treating queer individuals unfairly in social, professional, or legal contexts based on their sexual orientation or gender identity.
- **Stereotyping**: Perpetuating harmful stereotypes about queer individuals, such as viewing them as abnormal, deviant, or morally inferior.
- **Exclusion**: Marginalizing queer individuals within both heterosexual and LGBTQ+ communities, often leading to feelings of isolation.
- **Invisibility**: Ignoring or minimizing the presence and contributions of queer individuals in media, culture,

and discussions about sexuality and gender.

Queerphobia can have serious psychological and social impacts on individuals, contributing to mental health issues, social exclusion, and reduced quality of life. It is important to address and combat queerphobia through education, advocacy, and supportive policies to promote acceptance and equality for all individuals, regardless of their sexual orientation or gender identity. Queerphobia can be compounded by being Black or a POC, leading to what is known as intersectional discrimination. This concept, first introduced by legal scholar Kimberlé Crenshaw, describes how different aspects of a person's identity can overlap and create unique experiences of oppression and discrimination.

R

Race (1): To acknowledge race is a social fabrication, created to classify people on the arbitrary basis of skin color and other physical features. Although race has no genetic or scientific basis, the concept of race is important and consequential. Societies use race to establish and justify systems of power, privilege, disenfranchisement, and oppression".

Race (2): The fictional categories of people divided by origin and physical features that have nothing to do with biology.

Racial Gaslighting: A form of psychological manipulation that denies, questions, or minimizes the experiences of people of color and their perceptions of racism. It can make people of color feel like they are exaggerating, overly sensitive, or even crazy.

Example: "Her manager dismissed her concerns about racial comments, saying she was being too sensitive."

Racial Identity: Understanding how our identities and experiences have been shaped by race is vital. We are all awarded certain privileges and or disadvantages because of our race whether we are conscious of it or not. Racial identity is externally imposed: How do others perceive me? Racial identity is also internally constructed: How do I identify myself?

Example: This is where biracial people get confused. They may want to identify as half white and half other but there is no room for that in the system. White supremacy, the system that created racial identity, is an either/or machine with no in-between.

Racial Micro-Aggression: Racial microaggressions are brief and commonplace daily verbal, behavioral, or environmental indignities, whether intentional or unintentional, that communicate hostile, derogatory, or negative racial slights and insults toward people of color. Perpetrators of microaggressions are often unaware that they engage in such communications when they interact with racial/ethnic minorities.

Racialized: To give a racial character to; to categorize, marginalize, or regard according to race.

Racism: The systemic oppression of a racial group for the social, economic, and political benefit of another; a political and/or social system designed to execute principles of white supremacy.

Readulin: Effective intellectual treatment that requires books and comprehension of technical terms learned in master's classes (Veronica Gunn, Whitabetes Foundation, Founder).

Religion: A body of beliefs and practices regarding the supernatural and the worship of one or more deities.

Respectability Politics: A set of beliefs holding that conformity to prescribed mainstream standards of appearance and behavior will protect a person who is part of a marginalized group, especially a Black person, from prejudices and systemic injustices.

S

Self-Aware: Being aware of one's own personality or individuality. Self-awareness involves monitoring our stress, thoughts, emotions, and beliefs. It is important because it's a major mechanism influencing personal development.

Self-Preservation: Preservation of oneself from destruction or harm.

Sex: The physical difference between living beings who are male, female, and intersex (e.g., anatomy does not fit into "male" or "female").

Sexism: Behavior, conditions, or attitudes that foster stereotypes of social roles based on sex; prejudice or discrimination based on sex.

Social: Of or relating to human society, the interaction of the individual and the group, or the welfare of human beings as members of society; living and breeding in more or less organized communities especially for the purposes of cooperation and mutual benefit.

Spiritual: Related or joined in spirit; of or relating to supernatural beings or phenomena; of, relating to, consisting of, or affecting the spirit.

Stereotype: A generalized feeling and/or statement about all members of a group or all instances of a situation

Example: "Asian people are good at math."

Structural Racism: The overarching system of racial bias across institutions and society. These systems give privileges to white people resulting in disadvantages to people of color.

Superspreaders: An event or location at which a significant number of people contract the same communicable disease; an individual who is highly contagious and capable of transmitting a communicable disease to an unusually large number of uninfected individuals.

System: A regularly interacting or interdependent group of items forming a unified whole; a form of social, economic, or political organization or practice; an organized society or social situation regarded as stultifying or oppressive.

Systemic: Relating to a system, especially as opposed to a particular part; part of or embedded in the system.

Example: Keeping Black families out of white neighborhoods.

Systematic: Done or acting according to a fixed plan or system; methodical; following a system.

Example: Not able to secure a mortgage or having a mortgage with a high interest rate.

T

Token: A human being used as a tool to appear as an "ally" to a marginalized community; a human hired to appear anti-[insert virus] and/or diverse that will help secure grants/funding that at times are used to create jobs, salaries, and titles for people who have no interest or experience in running an equitable organization/agency. This happens in political and government positions.

Tokenism: Using a person or group that is marginalized as a shield or veil to hide and distract from their [virus]; "Generally speaking, tokenism is about including someone in a group purely for the sake of sounding or looking diverse. Tokenism is not sincere: Instead, it's keeping up looks and is superficial" (!Kaye Kaye).

Example: "I grew up in a Black neighborhood, or my [insert relationship to Black person] is Black.

Trans-racial: A term used to describe a Black (or other racialized group) child who was adopted (trafficked) to a white family suffering from white saviorism; a child who was trafficked to satisfy the emotional need of a white woman.

Transphobia: Irrational fear of, aversion to, or discrimination against transgender people.

U

V

Victim Mentality: A person who takes no accountability for their own actions and blames everyone but themselves. Signs include feeling powerless against problems in your life, feeling attacked when someone tries to offer helpful feedback, feeling bad for yourself gives you relief or pleasure, and feeling blame others for your circumstances.

Example: " I didn't create the system of racism so I can't do anything about."

W

White American Vernacular English (WAVE): The language of the Colonese translated in various forms of micro and macro aggressions and appropriated AAVE.

Example: "Educate me", "That's not racist I'm 16% Black", "chilly", the appropriated AAVE phrase of "Chile".

White Accountability: A myth; it refers to the collective and individual rejection of the existence of racism due to cognitive dissonance, white comfort, and delusions. This also contributes to their victim mentality.

Whitabetic Shock: The confusion experienced by white people when Black people reject their demands, racism, and authority (Veronica Gunn, Whitabetes Foundation, Founder).

Whitabetic Coma: The opposite of being "woke"; a state of most white people who have never left the protection and safety of living in the fantasy world of white supremacy and have no desire to wake up (Veronica Gunn, Whitabetes Foundation, Founder).

Whicessorising: When a white person (typically white women) uses their biracial children as accessories until they can no longer treat them like the

Black doll they wanted as a child. Another example is when white people adopt nonwhite children and build a profitable platform off their white saviorism (Veronica Gunn, Whitabetes Foundation, Founder).

Whikosis: A mental disorder causing complete detachment from the reality of being white and the reality of the abuse experienced by Black people or any racialized group (Veronica Gunn, Whitabetes Foundation, Founder).

Whitrums: The emotional and/or physical reactions of white people when they aren't centered and prioritized (Veronica Gunn, Whitabetes Foundation, Founder).

Example: The reaction of some white people to a Black Little Mermaid.

White (People): Having origins in any of the original peoples of Europe, the Middle East, or North Africa.

White Biracial: Individuals who do not present as their racialized (Asian, Black, Pacific Islander, Indigenous) side.

Example: Pete Wentz and Rashida Jones.

White Ego: According to Eric S. Piotrowski, it "…tells us that we understand the world very well. It tells us that our blind spots don't exist, or don't matter. It allows us to center our experience as a natural and complete lens through which the world should be filtered".

White Praise: When white people do the bare minimum, like donating to a racial justice cause, telling a family member not to use the "n-word" around Black people, or forcing themselves to watch Django for Black History Month.

White Rage: The violent reaction of white people when they feel their power, privilege, or white dominance is threatened. The reactions range from calling someone a racial slur to the events of January 6th.

White Savior: A white person who acts in a way that suggests they are rescuing non-white people from their plight, often with condescension or a sense of superiority.

White Supremacy: The lie created to place and keep white people, collectively as the superior race with the white man at the top. Over hundreds of years, white people created and maintain systems that enable them to oppress other groups that are not white, Christian, and/or straight.

White Tears: The emotional reaction of a white person when they are not centered, comforted, or are called out for racism. White women have used white tears to fuel rage in their husbands, brothers, fathers, uncles, and sons to torture, lynch, and murder innocent Black people.

White Womaning/Manning: When a white person demands education, exhibits white tears, and/or white rage and other behaviors like a toddler when they aren't centered (Veronica Gunn, Whitabetes Foundation, Founder).

Whilight Zone: Living in a mythical reality that defies the logic of social standards and acknowledgement of the White supremacy that afflict the world. This often affects all Whitabetics who cannot recognize or who disregard the oppression of White supremacy.

Whitelusions: Beliefs and ideas about social constructs that have been debunked with indisputable evidence. Chemical stabilization does not work with this symptom. The only thing that helps is intellectual therapy, but that may not work due to impenetrable blocks (Veronica Gunn, Whitabetes Foundation, Founder).

Whitesplaining: To comment on the minority experience or explain racism to a person of color in a condescending or blaming way, often pointing out accommodating behaviors that the victim of racism might have adopted to defuse interracial conflict.

Woke: Being conscious and aware of the undercurrents of social injustices.

X

Xenophobia: fear, hatred, or mistrust of people from other countries or cultures. It often manifests as hostility against foreigners or perceived outsiders, based on the belief that they are a threat to one's own social, economic, or cultural security. Xenophobia is not the same as racism and garners its own variation of understanding.

Y

Z

Made in the USA
Las Vegas, NV
14 October 2024

96885628R00067